THE STORY OF MARTIN LUTHER KING JR.

A Biography Book for New Readers

Written by
Christine Platt

Illustrated by
Steffi Walthall

ROCKRIDGE
PRESS

For everyone continuing Martin's great work—thank you.

Interior Designer: Amanda Kirk
Cover Designer: Stephanie Sumulong
Art Producer: Karen Williams
Editor: Eliza Kirby
Production Editor: Rachel Taenzler

Illustration © Steffi Walthall, pp. iv, 1, 4, 8, 11, 14, 16, 19, 20, 23, 26, 27, 30, 33, 34, 36, 38, 40, 43, 44, 49; Creative Market/Semicircular pp. 3, 13, 18, 29, 31, 41, 46; World History Archive / Alamy Stock Photo, p. 51; RBM Vintage Images / Alamy Stock Photo, p 53; Archive PL / Alamy Stock Photo, p 54; Author photo courtesy of © Nora E. Jones Photography; Illustrator photo courtesy of © Clarence Goss.

ISBN: Print 978-1-64152-954-9 | eBook 978-1-64152-955-6

R02

Printed in China

CONTENTS

CHAPTER 1
A KING IS BORN

Meet ★ Martin Luther King Jr. ★

As a young boy, Martin Luther King Jr. wanted to be a fireman. Then, a doctor. He loved singing and even considered being a performer. But Martin never thought he'd be a **civil rights** leader.

When Martin was born, the United States was a **segregated** country. Black and white **citizens** did almost everything separately. Their families often lived in different neighborhoods. Their children even went to different schools. Whenever they had to do things together, like ride the bus, black people were not treated fairly.

Even as a child, Martin knew **segregation** was wrong. He believed everyone deserved to be treated equally. When Martin became an adult, he would help lead the **civil rights movement** to end segregation.

How did Martin go from dreaming of being a fireman to giving his famous "I Have a Dream" speech? What inspired him to end segregation and fight for **equality**? Let's find out more about Martin's life and how he changed America.

> "There was a pretty strict system of segregation in Atlanta. For a long, long time I could not go swimming. . . ."

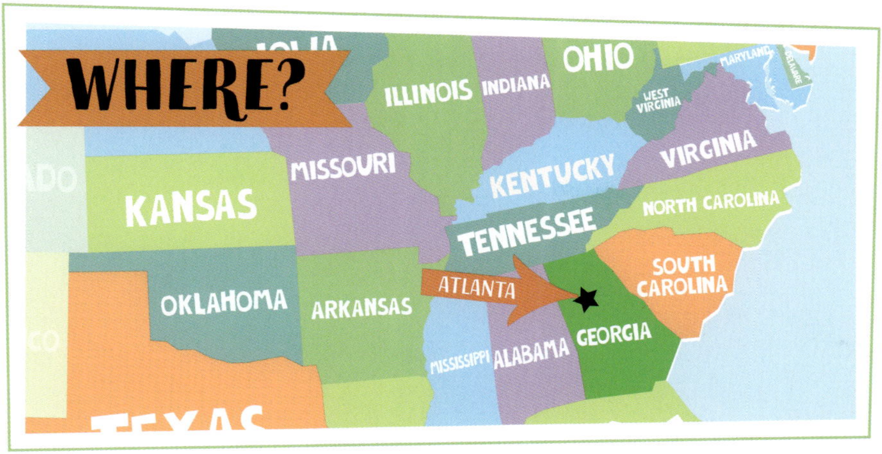

★ Martin's America ★

Martin was born on January 15, 1929, in Atlanta, Georgia. He was named after his father, **Reverend** Martin Luther King Sr., a popular minister at Ebenezer Baptist Church. Martin's mother, Alberta, trained as a schoolteacher.

More than 60 years before Martin was born, **slavery** was legal in the South. It was one of the main reasons the Civil War began on April 12, 1861, when Abraham Lincoln was president. The North wanted to end slavery and fought against the South. One of President Lincoln's goals was

to end slavery once and for all. He did many things to make this happen, including signing the **Emancipation Proclamation**.

The North won the Civil War, and slavery ended in 1865. The United States then began its **Reconstruction Era**. During this time, southern states created **Black Codes** and **Jim Crow laws**. These were rules that required black citizens to do most things separately from white citizens. Even if black workers did the same job as white workers, black workers were paid less. Over time, these laws became segregation laws, which was a form of **racism**.

When Martin was born, segregation laws still existed. So he experienced racism in his life, even as a child. Martin's first best friend was a white boy. But the boy's father told them they couldn't

MYTH & FACT

MYTH: When slavery ended, black and white people lived together peacefully.

FACT: Even after slavery, black and white people lived segregated lives, especially in the southern states. Many white people in the South were angry that they had lost the right to enslave people and continued to treat black people poorly.

JUMP IN THE THINK TANK

How would you feel if you had to stop being friends with someone because of their skin color?

be friends anymore because Martin was black. Martin was confused. He told his mother, and she explained that this was how things were under segregation. Martin felt very sad. He hoped segregation would end, so he'd never have to lose another friend.

Martin's childhood experiences of racism played a big role in the type of leader he would become. His life played a big role in the type of country America would become, too.

WHEN?

The first African slaves arrive in Jamestown, VA.

1619

The Civil War begins.

APRIL
1861

The Civil War ends.

APRIL
1865

The 13th Amendment ends slavery.

DECEMBER
1865

Martin Luther King Jr. is born.

JANUARY
1929

CHAPTER 2

THE EARLY YEARS

Growing Up in Atlanta

Martin grew up in a segregated neighborhood known as Sweet Auburn. It was one of the richest black communities in Atlanta. The King family had a beautiful house. Martin lived there with his grandparents and parents, along with his older sister, Willie Christine, and his younger brother, Alfred Daniel.

King Family Tree

When the King children weren't helping at their family church, they played outside and spent time with their mother. Mrs. King taught Martin and his siblings how to read and write. She also taught them how to play the piano. The family loved singing **gospel** songs together.

As the son of a preacher, Martin spent a lot of time at Ebenezer Baptist Church. Reverend King could be strict at times, but Martin admired his father. He was the first person Martin saw fight back against racism. During his church sermons, Reverend King preached about the need to end segregation. He encouraged Martin and his siblings to do the same.

> "I don't care how long I have to live with this system, **I will never accept it.**"
>
> **–REVEREND MARTIN LUTHER KING SR.**

Following in ★ Martin Sr.'s Footsteps ★

From grade school to high school, Martin's teachers recognized that he was very bright. Martin even skipped a few grades and graduated from high school early. When he was only 15 years old, Martin enrolled in college! He also made time to play his favorite sports like baseball and football.

Martin was proud to be a student at Morehouse College, a **historically black college** for men. Several King men had attended Morehouse, including Martin's father and grandfather. At Morehouse, Martin decided to follow in his father's footsteps and become a minister.

After graduating in 1948, Martin enrolled in Crozer Theological Seminary in Chester, Pennsylvania, to study religion. For the first time, Martin was attending a school that was

MYTH & FACT

MYTH: Only grade schools were segregated.

FACT: Segregation didn't end in high school. Even higher education was segregated—black and white students often went to separate colleges and universities.

mostly white. He was one of 11 black students on the entire campus.

Martin worried his white classmates wouldn't see him as equal. What if they thought he wasn't smart? But soon he saw that they respected him. Martin was even voted class president!

During his studies at Crozer Seminary, Martin learned about several religious leaders. He came to admire the Indian leader Mahatma

JUMP IN THE THINK TANK

How do you think Martin felt when he first enrolled in Crozer Seminary? How do you think you would have felt?

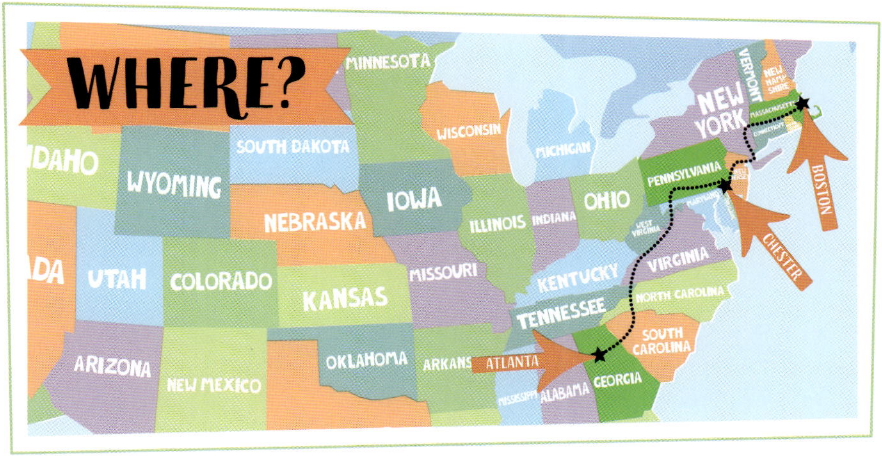

Gandhi. Martin liked Gandhi's **nonviolent** approach to social change.

After graduating from Crozer in 1951, Martin moved to Massachusetts to study at Boston University. Boston was a **diverse** city and did not have segregation laws. Students from different colleges often hung out together. That was how Martin met Coretta Scott, a student at the New England Conservatory of Music. They quickly fell in love and were married on June 18, 1953.

In 1954, Martin was offered a job at Dexter Avenue Baptist Church. He was excited to preach. He believed it was his calling. But Martin knew being a minister at this church wouldn't be easy. It was in Montgomery, Alabama—one of the most racist and segregated cities in the South.

WHEN?

1948 — Martin graduates from Morehouse College.

1951 — Martin graduates from Crozer Seminary and enrolls in Boston University.

1953 — Martin marries Coretta Scott.

1954 — Martin is offered a job at a church in Montgomery, Alabama.

CHAPTER 3

TAKING A STAND

Preaching for Equality

Martin and Coretta decided he should accept the job. Even though life was better for black people in the North, black communities in the South needed his help.

The moment Martin and Coretta arrived in Montgomery, they were reminded of the horrors of segregation. They had to drink from separate water fountains again. They had to ride in the backs of buses and sometimes give up their seats to white passengers. But Martin could finally preach about equality. In May 1954, Martin gave his first sermon as minister at the Dexter Avenue Baptist Church.

That same month, an important case was decided by the **Supreme Court**, the highest court in the United States. When a legal case is very difficult to decide, the Supreme Court

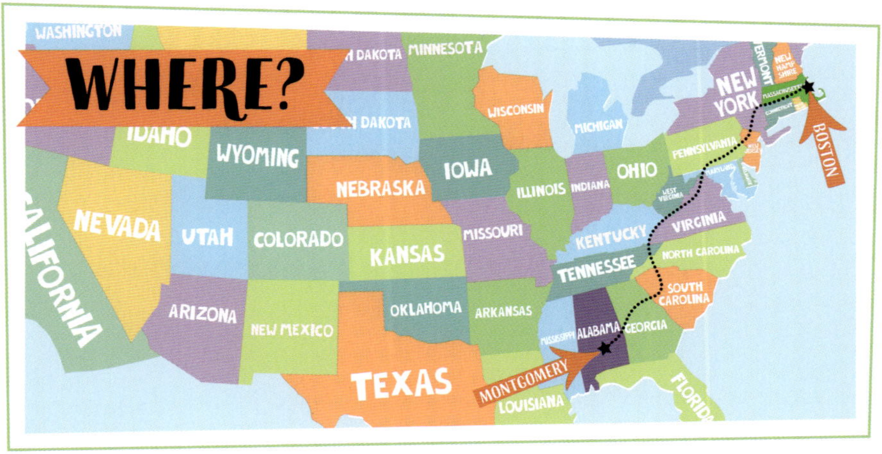

steps in to make a decision. In the case *Brown v. Board of Education,* several black families argued that segregated public schools were unfair and **unconstitutional**. On May 14, 1954, the Supreme Court agreed. This historic ruling meant that all public schools had to be **desegregated**.

Winning the right to attend the same schools as white students was just one of many segregation battles. In his sermons, Martin encouraged black residents in Montgomery to fight to end segregation—not just in schools, but everywhere. This was especially important to

Martin because on November 17, 1955, Coretta gave birth to their first child. Martin did not want his daughter, Yolanda Denise, to have to live through segregation.

★ Rosa Parks and the Montgomery Bus Boycott ★

Under segregation, black people had to sit in the backs of city buses. If there were not enough seats, black passengers had to give up their seats to white passengers. But black people were tired of being treated unfairly. They started refusing to move. Often, they were arrested. When Rosa Parks was arrested on December 1, 1955, for refusing to give up her seat, the black residents of Montgomery decided to take a stand.

Several of Montgomery's black leaders held a meeting. They decided to use Rosa Parks's arrest as a reason to **boycott** the city's buses. Martin was asked to lead the **Montgomery Bus Boycott**. Even though he knew it would be dangerous, Martin accepted. On December 5, 1955, black residents followed Martin's instructions—they refused to ride the city's buses unless they were desegregated.

JUMP IN THE THINK TANK

How would you feel if you were forced to give up your seat to someone else? Do you think you would have been as brave as Rosa Parks?

MYTH & FACT

MYTH: The Montgomery Bus Boycott didn't last a long time.

FACT: The Montgomery Bus Boycott began on December 5, 1955, and ended on December 20, 1956. Montgomery didn't agree to desegregate its buses for over a year!

Although the Montgomery Bus Boycott was difficult at times, it was a major success. Martin was thrilled that they had reached their goal without using violence.

But there was still work to be done. The civil rights movement was just getting started. There would be more difficult times ahead for citizens working for equal rights.

WHEN?

MAY 1954
The Supreme Court rules to desegregate public schools.

NOVEMBER 1955
Yolanda Denise King is born.

DECEMBER 1955
Rosa Parks is arrested and the Montgomery Bus Boycott begins.

DECEMBER 1956
The Montgomery Bus Boycott ends and public buses are desegregated.

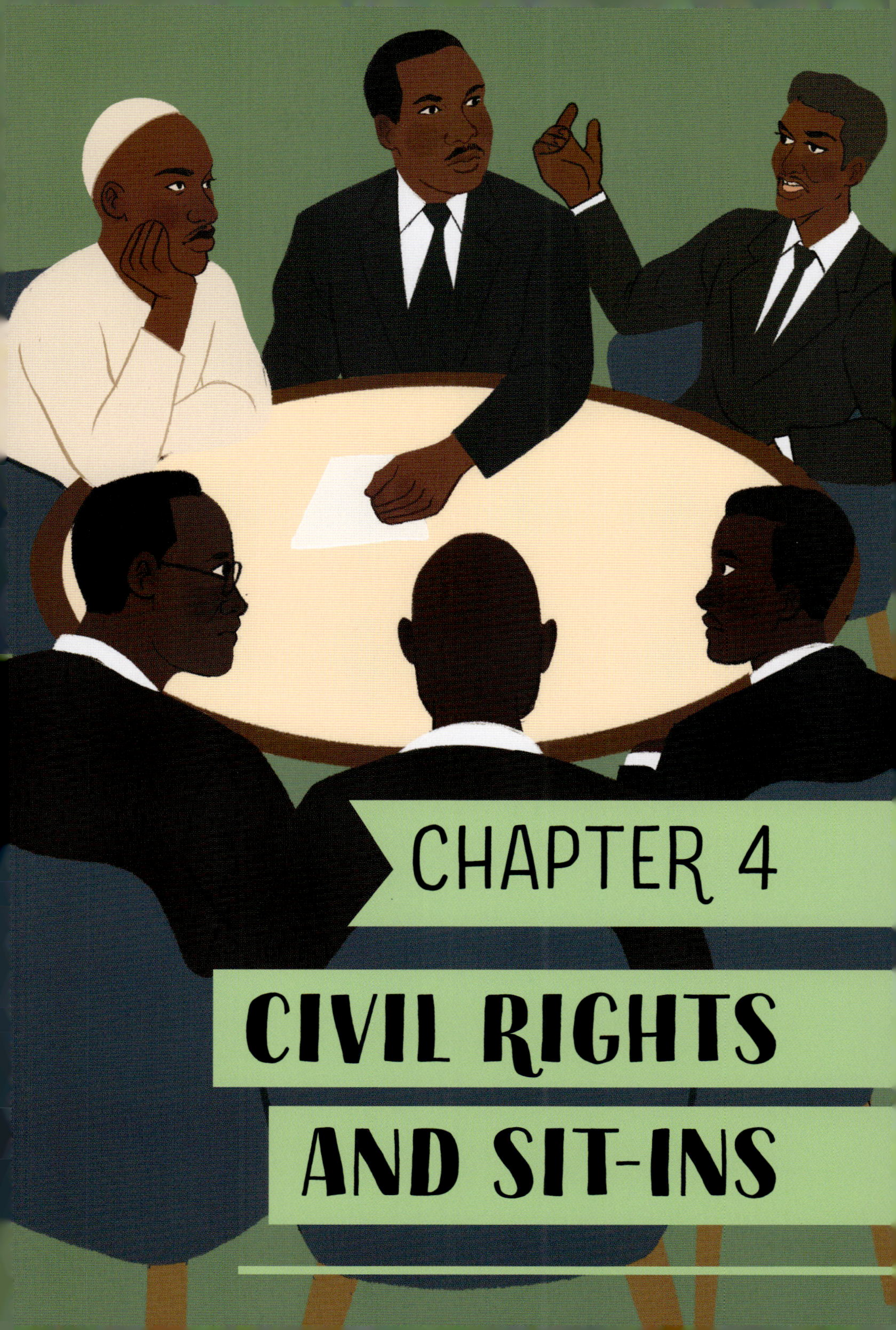

CHAPTER 4

CIVIL RIGHTS AND SIT-INS

★ Martin Leads the Way ★

The Montgomery Bus Boycott showed the power of peaceful protests against segregation. Soon they appeared throughout the South.

In January 1957, Martin went to Atlanta for a meeting with Bayard Rustin, Ralph Abernathy, Fred Shuttlesworth, and other black leaders. They formed the Southern Christian Leadership Conference (SCLC)—a civil rights organization. Martin was chosen as its president.

The SCLC also worked on other civil rights issues like voting. Their Crusade for Citizenship began in late 1957 to help register black voters. Martin went to a march in Washington, DC, called the Prayer Pilgrimage for Freedom and gave a speech called "Give Us the Ballot." In his speech, Martin told the crowd that black people were having trouble voting. He wanted to change that.

> "Give us the ballot,
> and we will no longer have to worry the federal government about our basic rights."

As the SCLC's president, Martin traveled a lot. But he returned to Montgomery often to be with his family. On October 23, 1957, Yolanda became a big sister when Martin Luther King III was born.

★ Peaceful Protests ★

In the late 1950s, Martin and other black citizens still faced big challenges. When nine black students tried to **integrate** an all-white high school in Little Rock, Arkansas, people tried to stop them. Things got so bad that the president had to call in the **National Guard**, part of the US military, to keep the students safe.

Soon after, Martin published his first book,

Stride Toward Freedom, about the bus boycott. He celebrated with a book signing in New York, but something terrible happened. A stranger stabbed him with a letter opener! Luckily, Martin survived.

For many years, Martin had wanted to visit India. But he never had time. After his stabbing, Martin decided to *make* time. In February 1959, Martin and Coretta traveled to India. Martin became even more inspired by Mahatma Gandhi's life and teachings. When the couple returned, Martin started planning more nonviolent protests.

The Kings moved to Atlanta in 1960. Martin liked being closer to the SCLC's headquarters. The move also made it easier to spend time with his family. Martin was even able to serve as his father's co-pastor at Ebenezer—the same church he attended as a boy.

In Atlanta, Martin organized events like **sit-ins**. Sit-ins were nonviolent protests where people refused to move from segregated areas. Throughout

JUMP IN THE THINK TANK

Imagine being arrested for sitting in a public restaurant because you wanted everyone to be treated fairly. How do you think you would react?

the South, sit-ins were popular, especially in shops and restaurants.

Southern police officers knew Martin inspired others to protest. They tried to find reasons to arrest him. Once, he was put in a Georgia jail for driving with an Alabama license. Thankfully, a congressman named John F. Kennedy helped get Martin released. A few months later, Mr. Kennedy became the 35th president of the United States.

In addition to sit-ins, Martin and his supporters participated in other nonviolent protests. They took **Freedom Rides** from the North to the South to challenge segregated buses. They held civil rights marches in many cities. Despite being arrested and jailed many times, Martin refused to give up. He would continue the fight for equality.

WHERE?

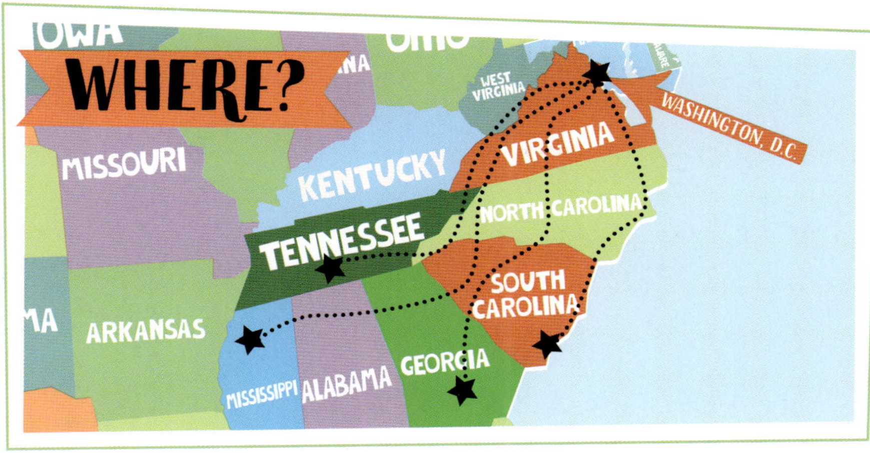

WHEN?

1957 — MLK helps found and lead the SCLC and Martin Luther King III is born.

1959 — The Kings move to Atlanta.

1960 — Sit-ins begin in Atlanta and spread throughout the South.

1961 — Freedom Rides begin and JFK becomes president.

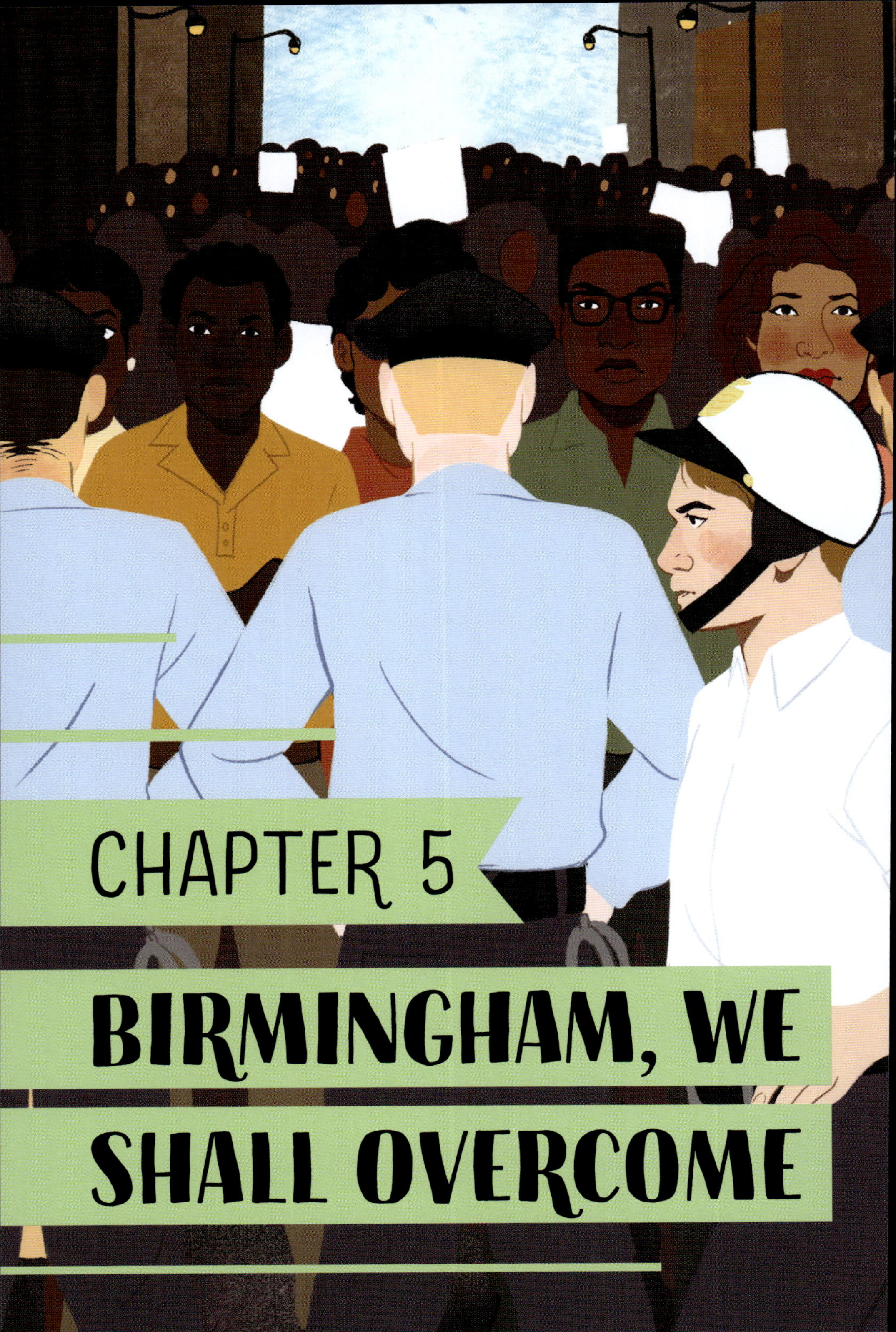

CHAPTER 5

BIRMINGHAM, WE SHALL OVERCOME

★ Birmingham Boycotts ★

In some places like Birmingham, Alabama, things were worse for black people than in other cities and states. In 1963, Alabama's new governor, George Wallace, made it known he did not want segregation to end. Birmingham's Commissioner of Public Safety, Eugene "Bull" Connor, declared that he didn't care if protests were peaceful—he would order police to use violence.

When Commissioner Connor heard the SCLC planned to come to Birmingham, he was furious.

JUMP IN THE THINK TANK

Would you have joined the Children's Crusade? Why or why not?

He made it **illegal** for Martin to protest there. Martin knew he risked being arrested and jailed. But he decided to protest anyway. He knew it was the right thing to do.

Birmingham's black residents were excited Martin was coming. Hundreds of people planned to boycott white businesses. Teenagers and children planned a march called the Children's Crusade. But as they prepared for a peaceful protest, Commissioner Connor ordered police to spray the crowd with fire hoses. Police dogs attacked the protestors, too.

Many protestors were arrested along with Martin, including some of the young people from the Children's Crusade. As Martin sat in jail, he wrote a letter about how bad things were in the South. Martin's words were powerful—despite

what happened, he still did not believe in responding to violence with violence. His letter was read on national television. More people started to realize the need for change. Martin's "Letter from Birmingham Jail" is one of his most famous writings.

★ Change for Birmingham ★

The Birmingham Campaign began on April 3 and lasted over a month. Martin and his supporters refused to give up. The protests ended on May 10—after Birmingham's business leaders agreed to end segregation.

The Birmingham Campaign showed America just how bad racism was in the South. When the campaign finally ended, many former whites-only businesses had their first black customers. In June 1963, segregation signs like those that read "Whites Only" and "No Colored" began to be removed.

> "Injustice anywhere is a **threat to justice everywhere.**"

The Birmingham Campaign was a success for the civil rights movement. Martin and his supporters believed it was time to push for change in one of the most important cities in the nation—Washington, DC.

WHEN?

APRIL 3 1963
Birmingham Campaign begins.

APRIL 7 1963
Police use violence on protestors.

APRIL 12 1963
Martin is arrested.

APRIL 16 1963
Martin writes "Letter from Birmingham Jail."

MAY 2 1963
Children's Crusade begins; more than 1,000 children arrested.

MAY 10 1963
Birmingham Campaign ends; Birmingham begins desegregation.

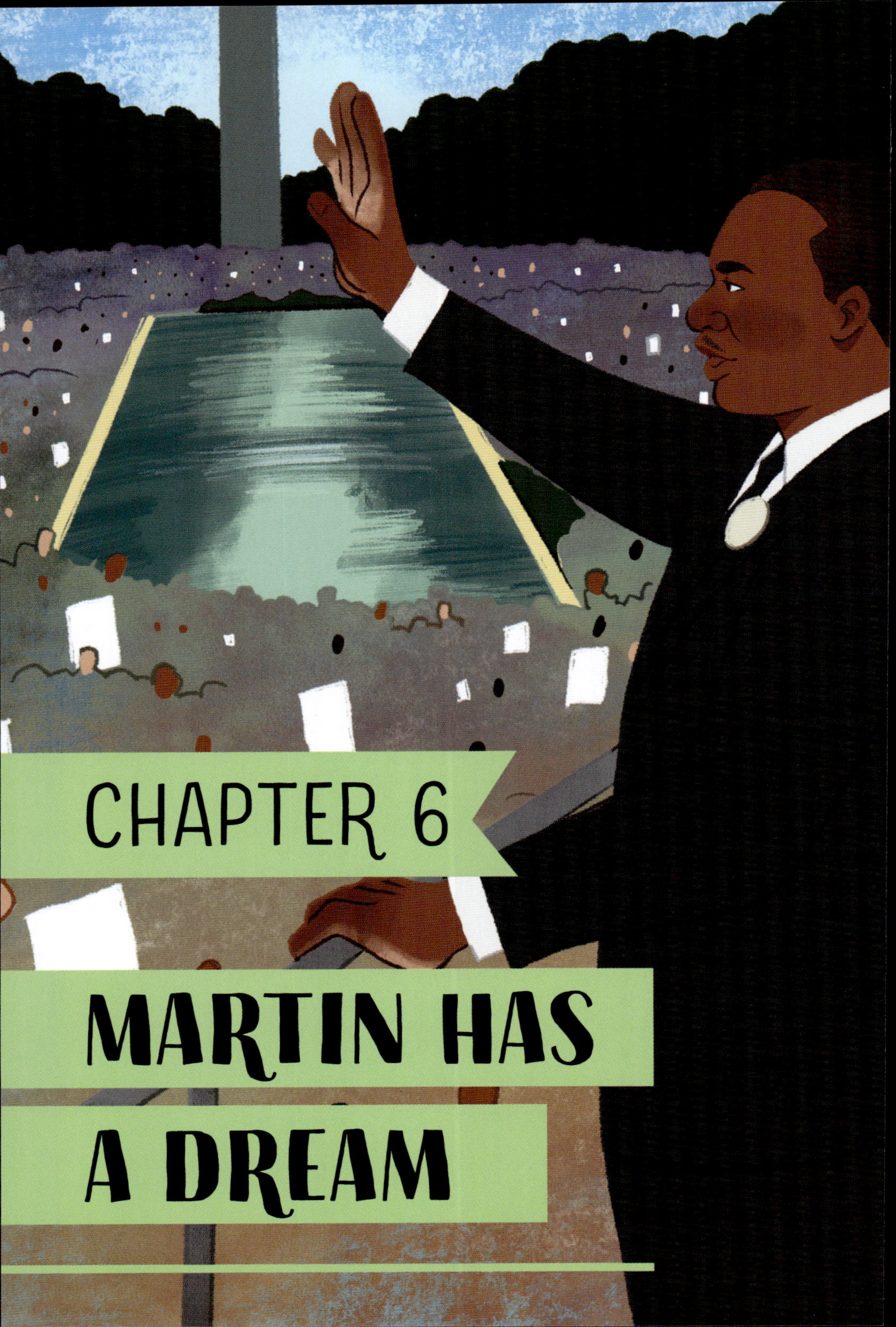

CHAPTER 6
MARTIN HAS A DREAM

Marching on Washington, DC

Martin knew he had support in Washington. John F. Kennedy, the man who'd helped get him released from jail, was now president of the United States. President Kennedy also believed in equality. On June 11, 1963, he gave a powerful speech about the violence that had happened in Birmingham a few months before. President Kennedy encouraged all citizens to work together to bring about change.

On June 19, President Kennedy introduced a new civil rights bill to Congress. If passed, the law would end segregation in public places like schools and restaurants forever. Martin's efforts to promote this bill would lead to his most famous speech.

Martin worked with other leaders to plan an event called the March on Washington for Jobs and Freedom. Many people helped plan the march, but Martin worked closely with five other leaders. Together, they were called the Big Six.

MLK: Chairman, SCLC

John Lewis: President, Student Nonviolent Coordinating Committee

A. Philip Randolph: Labor Union Organizer

Roy Wilkins: Executive Director, NAACP

James Farmer: Founder, CORE

Whitney Young: Executive Director, National Urban League

On June 22, 1963, the Big Six met with President Kennedy to discuss their plans. They promised the event would be nonviolent. President Kennedy gave his support, and the March on Washington for Jobs and Freedom was scheduled for August 28, 1963.

> "It ought to be possible . . . for every American to enjoy the privileges of being American without regard to his race or his color."
>
> –**PRESIDENT KENNEDY**

Over 250,000 people came in support of the March on Washington. Around 80,000 of these supporters were white people. Strangers linked arms as they marched and sang together. It was the largest showing of racial **unity** America had ever seen.

JUMP IN THE THINK TANK

How might today's world be different if MLK and his thousands of followers hadn't marched in Washington in support of civil rights?

After several people gave performances and speeches, Martin addressed the audience. He shared with them his dreams for America. Martin's "I Have a Dream" speech is one of the most quoted speeches in the world.

The March on Washington ended as the crowd sang the anthem of the Civil Rights Movement, "We Shall Overcome." The time for change had come.

> One day . . . little black boys and black girls will be able to join hands with little white boys and white girls as sisters and brothers.

★ Change for America ★

Sadly, President Kennedy died before seeing the rewards of his work. When he was **assassinated** on November 22, 1963, the nation mourned. On July 2, 1964, President Lyndon B. Johnson

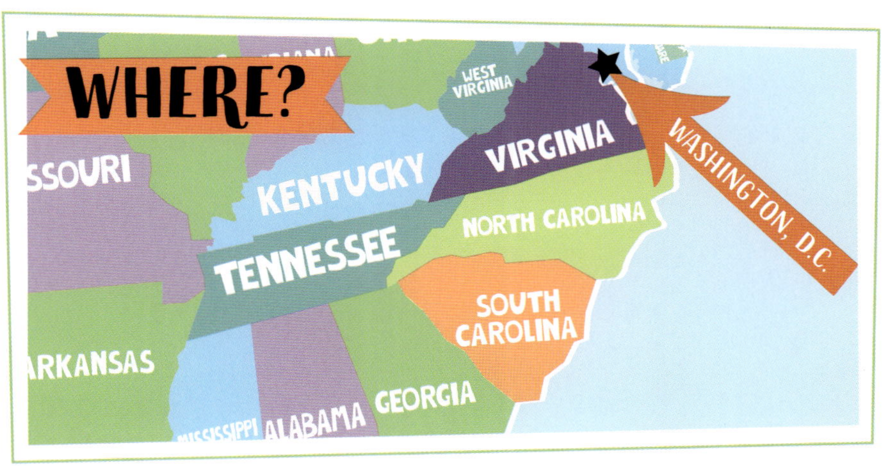

signed the Civil Rights Bill of 1964, honoring President Kennedy. After the tireless work of many civil rights leaders and their supporters, segregation had ended in the United States. Martin was proud and thankful.

On October 14, 1964, Martin was awarded the prestigious **Nobel Peace Prize**. At 35 years old, he is among the youngest people to ever win the prize. But Martin's work wasn't finished just yet. There was still a lot more he wanted to do—for himself and the nation.

WHEN?

The March on Washington takes place.	JFK is assassinated.	The Civil Rights Bill of 1964 is passed.	MLK receives the Nobel Peace Prize.
AUGUST **1963**	NOVEMBER **1963**	JULY **1964**	OCTOBER **1964**

CHAPTER 7

FIGHTING UNTIL THE END

★ Marching from Selma to Montgomery ★

After the Civil Rights Act of 1964 was passed, people expected things to get better right away. But they didn't. Some cities chose to close schools rather than desegregate them. Other cities had unfair rules that made it hard for black citizens to register to vote.

One of those cities was Selma, Alabama. On March 7, 1965, several civil rights activists tried to peacefully march from Selma to Montgomery to protest unfair voting rules. They were met with violence from **state troopers**. The march and violence were broadcast on television. It was so bad that the day became known as Bloody Sunday.

JUMP IN THE THINK TANK

By 1965, Martin had worked so hard, he could have easily decided to take a break and let someone else continue his fight. Why do you think he didn't stop?

People were very upset, including Martin. On March 21, he led a second march from Selma to Montgomery. This time, the peaceful protestors had protection from the Alabama National Guard. There was no violence. The 54-mile march took five days. Martin began with a small crowd of supporters. But by the time they reached Montgomery, the crowd had grown to 25,000 people! Martin was excited that so many

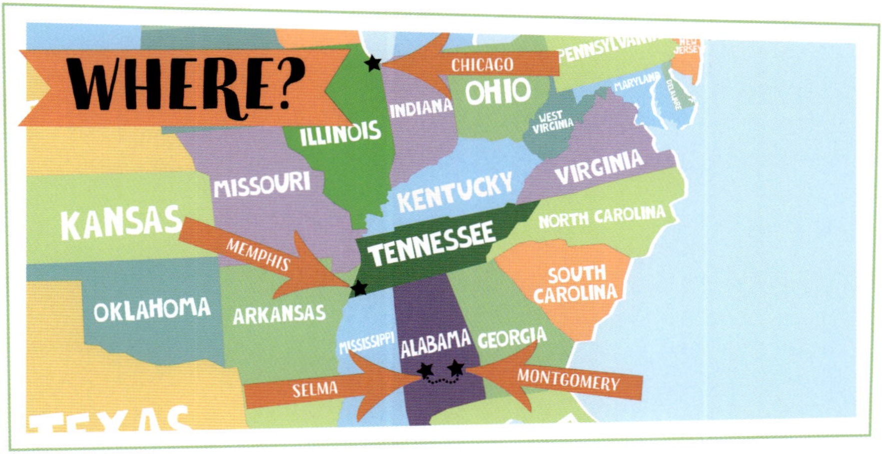

people supported equal voting rights.

The march made a big impact on President Lyndon Johnson. On August 6, he signed the Voting Rights Act of 1965, which ended unfair rules that made it hard for black citizens to vote. It was a historic moment for Martin and the country.

★ A Tragic Goodbye ★

Martin achieved many of his goals for equality. But rather than rest, Martin continued to speak out when he saw injustice. Martin protested war and **poverty**, and fought for **equal housing rights**.

> “Justice is love correcting that which revolts against love.”

Coretta and their children continued to support his important work.

In April 1968, Martin went to Memphis, Tennessee, to help black sanitation workers. They were protesting to be paid the same as white workers. Sadly, it would be Martin’s last protest. On April 4, 1968, Martin’s life ended when he was assassinated standing on the balcony of the Lorraine Motel in Memphis. The man who killed him, James Earl Ray, was a racist who did not believe in equality. After the assassination, James Earl Ray went on the run. He was finally captured on July 19, 1968. He pleaded guilty to Martin’s murder and was sentenced to 99 years in prison.

Throughout the world, people were saddened by Martin's tragic death. Thousands went to his funeral in Atlanta. A few days later, President Johnson honored Martin by signing the Civil Rights Act of 1968. This law fulfilled one of Martin's last goals for equal housing rights. If people wanted to rent or buy property, it was illegal to discriminate against them because of their race, religion, or nationality.

Even though Martin's life ended, people continued to support his dream, especially Coretta. In 1968, she created The King Center in Atlanta. Every year, hundreds of thousands of people visit to honor Martin's legacy.

Martin is forever remembered as one of the world's greatest civil rights leaders. In 1977, he was awarded the Presidential Medal of Freedom, and in 2004, a Congressional Gold Medal. Today, people from all over the world travel to Washington, DC, to visit the Martin Luther King, Jr. Memorial.

WHEN?

The Voting Rights Act is passed.

1965

The Kings move to Chicago, Illinois.

1966

MLK is assassinated and the Civil Rights Act of 1968 is passed.

1968

CHAPTER 8

SO . . . WHO WAS MARTIN LUTHER KING JR.?

★ Challenge Accepted! ★

Now that you have learned how Martin Luther King Jr. dedicated his life to ensure every American has equal rights and opportunities, let's test your new knowledge in a little who, what, when, where, why, and how quiz. Feel free to look back in the text to find the answers if you need to, but try to remember first!

1 Where was Martin born?

→ A Montgomery
→ B Selma
→ C Atlanta
→ D Boston

2 What college did Martin attend when he was 15 years old?

→ A Morehouse College
→ B Crozer Theological Seminary
→ C Boston University
→ D Martin didn't attend college when he was 15 years old.

3 **What Indian activist did Martin admire?**

→ A President John F. Kennedy

→ B Mahatma Gandhi

→ C John Lewis

→ D Rosa Parks

4 **Where did Martin meet his wife, Coretta Scott?**

→ A Atlanta

→ B Selma

→ C Montgomery

→ D Boston

5 **What was the name of the first church that hired Martin as a minister?**

→ A Ebenezer Baptist Church

→ B Dexter Avenue Baptist Church

→ C Montgomery Baptist Church

→ D Boston Avenue Baptist Church

6 What boycott ended segregation on city buses?

- A The Birmingham Campaign Bus Boycott
- B The Montgomery Bus Boycott
- C The Selma Bus Boycott
- D The Atlanta Bus Boycott

7 Martin served as the president of which civil rights organization?

- A Southern Christian Leadership Conference
- B Northern Christian Leadership Conference
- C Students Against Nonviolence Coordinating Committee
- D Civil Rights Society

8 What was the name of the speech that Martin gave at the March on Washington for Jobs and Freedom?

- A "Give Us the Ballot"
- B "I Have a Dream"
- C "I Believe"
- D "Here in Washington"

9 **How many miles did Martin and his supporters march in support of black voting rights in Selma?**

→ A 10 miles
→ B 25 miles
→ C 45 miles
→ D 54 miles

10 **How was Martin honored for his civil rights work?**

→ A Nobel Peace Prize
→ B Congressional Gold Medal
→ C Presidential Medal of Freedom
→ D All of the above

Answers: 1. A, 2. A, 3. B, 4. D, 5. B, 6. B, 7. A, 8. B, 9. D, 10. D

★ Our World ★

The benefits of Martin's work can still be seen today:

- → Civil rights organizations continue to follow Martin's approach to change through nonviolence and peaceful protests.
- → People continue to live by Martin's words: *Injustice anywhere is a threat to justice everywhere.*
- → More people speak out against injustice rather than stay silent. They often do so in Martin's name and honor.
- → Martin's life continues to inspire people to work toward achieving their dreams, no matter how impossible they might seem.

JUMP IN THE THINK TANK FOR MORE!

Now let's think a little more about what Martin Luther King Jr. did, and how his actions affected our world.

→ How do you see Martin's work reflected in your life? Think about your school and where you live.

→ Martin's "I Have a Dream" speech inspired many people to make the world a better place. What kind of a world do you dream of living in?

→ What are some ways that you can continue Martin's dream for equal rights and opportunities for everyone?

Glossary

assassinate: To kill someone, usually a leader, by sudden or secret attack

Black Codes: Laws in the South designed to restrict black people's rights and freedoms after slavery ended

boycott: Refusal to deal with a person, store, or organization until certain conditions are met, agreed to, or both

citizen: A person who legally lives in and belongs to a country

civil rights: The rights that are granted to every citizen to be treated fairly and equally

civil rights movement: The fight to end racial discrimination in the United States so black people could have equal rights and be treated fairly

desegregate: To end laws, policies, or both that enforce racial segregation

diverse: Having a variety of something, particularly a variety of different people

Emancipation Proclamation: An order by President Abraham Lincoln that freed all enslaved people in 1863

equal housing rights: The ability to rent, own, or live in property without discrimination

equality: When every person has the same rights and opportunities

Freedom Rides: A form of nonviolent protest where activists rode buses from the North into the South

gospel: A style of music most often sung in black churches, especially in southern Baptist churches

historically black colleges and universities: Schools established under segregation to serve African-American students

illegal: Against the law

integrate: To end segregation

Jim Crow laws: Laws that enforced racial segregation following the end of slavery

Montgomery Bus Boycott: A campaign to end racial segregation on city buses in Montgomery, Alabama

National Guard: A state military force; can also be used by the federal government in emergencies

Nobel Peace Prize: An international prize awarded every year for outstanding work in the promotion of peace

nonviolent: Peaceful or without using physical force, especially as a way to bring about social change

poverty: The state of being very poor

racism: Discrimination against someone of a different race based on the belief that one's own race is superior

Reconstruction Era: The period that followed the American Civil War and during which America had to change its laws, especially for formerly enslaved black people

reverend: A title given to the leader of a church

segregation: The separation of people, usually based on their race or skin color

sit-in: A peaceful protest in which people refuse to leave a place until their demands are met

slavery: When a person has little or no freedom and is forced to work against their will; a labor system used in America that primarily used black people for work and other services against their will

state troopers: Police officers who are members of their state police force

Supreme Court: The highest federal court in the United States whose nine justices have the power to hear and rule on all other state and local court cases

unconstitutional: When an action, law, or policy goes against the rights granted to every citizen

unity: The state of coming together; the state of people joining together

Bibliography

Bolden, Tonya. *M.L.K. Journey of a King.* New York: Abrams Books for Young Readers, 2006.

Carson, Clayborne. *The Martin Luther King, Jr., Encyclopedia.* Westport, CT: Greenwood Press, 2008.

Carson Clayborne and Kris Shepard eds. *A Call to Conscience: The Landmark Speeches of Dr. Martin Luther King, Jr.* New York: Warner Books, 2001.

"Congressional Gold Medal for Martin Luther King, Jr. and Coretta Scott King," National Museum of African American History and Culture, Smithsonian Institution, Washington, DC., accessed April 4, 2020, NMAAHC.SI.edu/object/nmaahc_2014.135ab.

King, Jr., Martin Luther. *The Autobiography of Martin Luther King, Jr.* Edited by Clayborne Carson. London: Abacus, 1998.

The Martin Luther King, Jr. Research and Education, accessed March 2020, kinginstitute.stanford.edu/institute/king-institute.

National Park Service, "March on Washington for Jobs and Freedom. Last updated August 10, 2017." nps.gov/articles/march-on-washington.htm.

Siebold, Thomas, ed. *Martin Luther King, Jr.* San Diego, CA: Greenhaven Press, 2000.

About the Author

CHRISTINE PLATT is a literacy activist and passionate advocate for educational justice and policy reform. She holds a B.A. in Africana Studies from the University of South Florida, an M.A. in African and African American Studies from The Ohio State University, and a J.D. from Stetson University College of Law. A believer in the power of storytelling as a tool for social change, Christine's literature centers on teaching history, race, equity, diversity, and inclusion to people of all ages.

About the Illustrator

STEFFI WALTHALL is an illustrator and character designer who has always been inspired by strong, fearless women, whether in history or in fiction. Steffi loves human-centric stories and creating images that celebrate and embrace diversity (and usually include a lady with a sword). When not working on a project, she can be found searching for inspiration in a book or out in nature with her Polaroid camera looking for another story to begin.

WHO WILL INSPIRE YOU NEXT?

EXPLORE A WORLD OF HEROES AND ROLE MODELS IN ***THE STORY OF***... BIOGRAPHY SERIES FOR NEW READERS.

LOOK FOR THIS SERIES

WHEREVER BOOKS AND EBOOKS ARE SOLD

Alexander Hamilton
Albert Einstein
Martin Luther King Jr.
George Washington
Jane Goodall
Barack Obama
Helen Keller
Marie Curie